The Diabetes Weight Loss Cookbook

Quick and Easy Recipes for Diabetes Type 1
and Type 2 incl. Weight Loss Journal

Matthew G. Thomson

ISBN - 9798656662970

TABLE OF CONTENTS

INTRODUCTION

What is diabetes?

Diabetes is a lifelong condition that damages your body's capability to process blood glucose, also known as blood sugar.

Unfortunately, diabetes is becoming all too common with an increasing number of people being diagnosed every day. It's estimated that around 30% of Americans struggle with this disease already and it has serious consequences on health, including an increased risk of stroke and heart disease.

Careful management and ongoing care are two very important factors for avoiding the build up of sugars in the blood. Diabetes is a serious disease and sadly, one that is not curable. However, we can treat it with both medicine and lifestyle changes.

People who suffer from it can expect to live a long and relatively healthy life, as long as they treat the disease and do not ignore the limitations it brings. In this book we will explore the disease in more detail and present plenty of delicious and healthy recipes, as well as a 10 day weight loss journal. Hopefully helping anyone that suffers from diabetes to maintain a healthy lifestyle and lose weight in the process.

About Diabetes

There are two main types of diabetes that people suffer from (type 1 and type 2) and we also recognise gestational diabetes and a condition known as pre-diabetes. Let's take a closer look at each one and explain the main differences.

Type 1 diabetes (also referred to as juvenile diabetes) is what causes the levels of sugar (glucose) in your blood to become too high. Your body simply stops producing enough of a hormone called insulin, which is in charge of controlling your blood glucose levels. It is common for this type of diabetes to be diagnosed very early in life.

Diabetes type 1 is an autoimmune disease. Your body essentially attacks itself and unlike type 2, it is not at all linked to age or weight. Sufferers of type 1 diabetes will need injections of insulin on a daily basis to keep it under control. There is no cure for it and it is a lifelong disease.

Type 2 diabetes is a very common condition and it causes your levels of sugar (glucose) in the system to become too high, causing problems with the hormone, insulin. It's often closely connected to being overweight or general inactivity, but can also be attributed to having diabetes type 2 in your family.

This too is a lifelong condition and it may seriously affect your life. You will most likely have to change your diet and your lifestyle, take medicine and go to a doctor on a regular basis.

The symptoms are excessive thirst, tiredness and a constant need to pee. If left untreated, it can cause problems with your heart, nerves or even your eyes. You should pay attention to the symptoms and address the issue as soon as possible. The earlier it's diagnosed and treated, the better.

Gestational diabetes, as the name suggests, is a condition that only effects pregnant women. It is a temporary condition that disappears after giving birth. It most commonly appears in the second or third trimester. Your body simply cannot make insulin fast enough for the extra needs that come with pregnancy. It can cause some issues for the mother and the baby, but the risk is greatly reduced if it's detected and treated early on. Women who have had gestational diabetes are more at risk from suffering from the condition in future pregnancies, as well as being more prone to developing type 2 diabetes later in life.

Pre-diabetes is a condition connected to high blood sugar levels, but not yet diagnosed as official type 2 diabetes. If ignored, this condition will almost certainly lead to diabetes. It will get worse through time, so again, early detection is key. The symptoms are mild and very general (increased thirst, frequent peeing), so it often goes undetected.

How do problems with insulin develop?

We do not know what causes type 1 diabetes, but type 2 diabetes has a more clear origin. It is also known as insulin resistance, which is usually a result of the following:

- Genes or an environment, which makes a person more unable to produce enough insulin for the amount of glucose they consume.

- There is an excess of blood glucose and the body tries to produce more insulin to process it.

- The pancreas can not adjust fast enough and the excess blood sugar starts circulating in your blood.

- Blood sugar levels increase over time and insulin becomes less effective.

This building resistance to insulin is a slow process in type 2 diabetes. That is why doctors suggest lifestyle changes in order to slow down or even reverse this cycle.

Who is at risk?

Type 1 diabetes can develop at any point in your life, but it is most commonly discovered and diagnosed in children and young adults. It is much rarer than type 2 diabetes. To this day we don't know how it can be prevented.

The symptoms can develop very quickly, in just a few weeks or even days, and can be very harmful. Risk factors are not very clear, but what we do know is that family history plays a part and that exposure to a trigger, such as a virus in the environment, can cause diabetes type 1 to develop.

Type 2 diabetes and pre-diabetes, on the other hand, have similar risk factors:

- Obesity
- High blood pressure
- Family history of diabetes
- Age (more than 45 years)
- Lack of exercise
- Being of Chinese, black African or South Asian origin

What are the symptoms and how to get diagnosed?

The symptoms for diabetes type 1 and type 2 are very similar. The most common symptoms being:

- A constant feeling of thirst
- Blurred vision
- Urinating often, particularly at night time
- Strong feeling of tiredness
- Unintentional weight loss
- Wounds and cuts that take a long time to heal
- Repeated thrush or itchiness around your vagina or penis

If you have any of the symptoms of diabetes or if you think you might be at risk, you should visit your General Practitioner. He or she will check your blood glucose levels and do a urine test and it should only take 1 to 2 days to get the results back. Your General Practitioner will usually ask you to fast (not eat or drink anything apart from water, black tea, or coffee) for 12 hours before the tests as this helps them assess the way your body is regulating insulin.

If you test positive for diabetes type 1, you will be referred to a hospital for assessment. A diabetes specialist will explain what the next steps are. You will have to learn how to create a healthy activity and eating plan and how to stick to it. You will also be taught how to test your levels of blood glucose, as well as how to take insulin, whether it be by pen, pump or syringe. You will also be educated on how to check your body for early signs of problems. Stress management is very important when first getting diagnosed and constant care will become part of your daily life.

If you test positive for diabetes type 2, you will be called back to your General Practitioner and he will explain what medicine you will have to take (if any), how you will have to change your diet and lifestyle. Following that, you will need to go back for regular check-ups and monitoring.

Staying healthy

Healthy lifestyle habits are really important for all of us, not just for people with diabetes. There is a lot we can do ourselves to help prevent or treat diabetes, if the condition has already developed. Here are 6 steps you can take to prevent or help manage diabetes:

Eat healthily

Eating healthily is one of the most important factors for a diabetic as your diet directly affects your blood sugar levels. Avoiding foods that are high in sugar (obviously) and fat are necessary to avoid blood sugar spikes. But remember, no foods are completely off limits. It is crucial that you watch your carbohydrates intake as carbs turn into sugar. Eat plenty of wholegrain foods, fresh fruit and especially vegetables. Focus on eating the thing and amounts that your body needs and do not overindulge.

Exercise

This is a very obvious lifestyle change. You should aim for a minimum 30 minutes of exercise or activity that make you breathe faster almost every day of the week. You don't need to go to the gym to achieve this, or buy an expensive membership. Go swimming, go for a walk, ride a bicycle, or even play video games where you have to stand up and be active. Regular exercise will help your diabetes by bringing down your blood sugar levels very quickly.

Manage your stress levels

Stress causes your blood sugar levels to go up. Find hobbies or activities that help you relax. You might not be able to monitor and manage your diabetes efficiently if you are under a lot of stress. You might accidentally skip meals, forget to exercise, forget to take your medicine, or be more inclined to eat unhealthy foods. You can practice mindfulness techniques to combat anxiety and there are many different ways to achieve that, for example yoga, breathing exercises, and meditation. You can also do all of these in your home, free of charge!

Visit your doctor at least twice a year

You need a check-up to assess how your diabetes is being managed and if you need to readjust the quantities of insulin you may or may not need to administer. Many people can actually control their type 2 diabetes just by diet and lifestyle changes alone! Have an eye exam every year with your local optometrist as they can take a picture of the back of your eyes and diagnose retinal degeneration quickly. If it goes untreated, it can cause blindness.

Quit smoking

Unfortunately, diabetes makes you more susceptible to other health conditions. Issues such as heart disease, eye disease, nerve damage, some types of cancer, vessel disease and many more. If you smoke, statistically you are already more at risk for these diseases and diabetes enhances this risk even further. Smoking can also make it more difficult for you to be active as it reduces your endurance. Speak with your general practitioner about quitting. There are many options available, from patches, vaping, nicotine gum and even hypnosis.

Reduce your alcohol intake

Many beers, wines and liquors contain very high quantities of sugar and carbohydrates. These additional calories can make it very hard for you to control your blood sugar levels. You can try switching out the more sugary liquors and beer for less sugary drinks, such as gin and tonic or vodka, soda and lime. However, alcohol intake usually lowers your inhibitions and might make it harder for you to practice self discipline and stick to your diet and exercise plan.

The importance of maintaining a healthy weight

Without a doubt we all know there are physical and emotional benefits to losing any extra weight you're carrying, but why is that so important to diabetics?

The answer is simple. If you are overweight, the fat can not only make you feel worse about yourself, but it has devastating consequences on your body. It can build up around your organs, for example your pancreas and your liver, and this is where insulin resistance can occur.

So, there are two major benefits of embarking on a healthy diet plan. The weight loss could help the insulin your body produces naturally, or at least help the artificial insulin you are injecting, to work properly. If you succeed, you and your medical team may have to reassess your medication intake, especially insulin. Needing less medication can also provide great motivation for losing extra weight!

As mentioned previously, type 1 diabetes doesn't have anything to do with weight. However, the healthier you are and the closer you are to your ideal weight, the better your chances are needing less insulin, plus the risk of health complications will be greatly reduced.

For type 2 diabetes, the reward can be even greater as reaching your ideal weight could put you into remission. This means you could potentially stop taking medication altogether!

So as you can see, there are fantastic health rewards to be gained from achieving and maintaining a healthy weight. You just need to create a meal and exercise plan and stick to it! The faster you reach your ideal weight, the better.

A healthy diet

A diabetes diet does not need to be very rigid and boring. A diet rich in complex carbohydrates can be very beneficial to all types of diabetics. Foods such as brown rice, oats, whole wheat, hemp, vegetables, beans and lentils are essential for keeping and maintaining your insulin levels at a stable and consistent range.

This is because these food types release their energy slowly and they are high in natural nutrients, such as fiber, vitamins, carbs and minerals. They have been proven to help keep your blood sugar under control.

Foods to avoid include simple carbohydrates, such as white sugar, white rice and bread, pastry, and pasta. These foods convert into sugar very quickly, causing your insulin levels to spike drastically.

Good food choices for diabetics:

Oily fish:

Salmon, mackerel, and herring are a wonderful and natural source of Omega 3 fatty acids. They have many major health benefits, especially for people who are at risk of developing heart disease or having a stroke. Fish is an incredible source of protein, which can help you feel full for longer, as well as help you avoid snacking throughout the day. They have also been proven to speed up your metabolism.

Green leafy vegetables:

Leafy greens are very low-calorie and provide an abundance of nutrients and vitamins, including vitamin C. It has been proven in trials that increasing your vitamin C intake can help reduce inflammation, as well as manage blood sugar levels and reduce high blood pressure. Vegetables, such as spinach, kale and rocket are also recommended because of the high level of antioxidants and iron they contain.

Diets, rich in leafy green vegetables can also help to protect your eyes from macular degeneration and cataracts, both of which can occur in people with diabetes more commonly than in non-diabetics.

Cinnamon:

Recently, studies have shown that cinnamon can improve insulin sensitivity and can lower blood sugar levels. It could also lower your cholesterol levels, but this needs to be investigated further. It can be a great addition to low sugar desserts or drinks, healthy smoothies and juices and it is also a popular spice used in curry dishes.

Eggs:

Eggs are an inexpensive way of adding healthy fats to your diet, as well as protein. They can be cooked in a range of different ways and keep you satisfied and fuller for longer. They improve a variety of risk factors and can promote good blood sugar control.

Chia seeds:

This is another great addition to a diabetic diet. Chia seeds are very high in fiber, but still low in digestive carbs. The healthy viscous fiber in chia seeds lowers blood sugar levels. It does this by slowing down how quickly food gets digested and how fast it's absorbed into your body. Foods high in fiber reduce hunger and make you feel full for longer which can help you achieve a healthy weight.

Turmeric:

Similar to cinnamon, turmeric is extremely healthy and easy to add to a lot of your meals. It lowers inflammation and reduces the risk of heart disease. In studies, turmeric appears to improve kidney function in diabetics. Unfortunately, diabetes can also cause kidney disease, so regular consumption of turmeric is advised for healthier kidneys

NB. When adding turmeric to your meals, you should also add some black pepper as it increases the bioavailability of turmeric by a whopping 2000%.

Greek yogurt

This is one of the best dairy choices for diabetics. It's low carb and high protein, which is very good for weight loss, especially for people with type 2 diabetes. High protein and good fats will reduce your appetite which will help you on your weight loss journey. Greek yoghurt is a healthy and filling addition to breakfast cereals, fruit salads, smoothies, and also works as a frozen dessert.

Extra virgin cold pressed olive oil

Olive oil is the only fats that is proven to lower the risk of heart disease. It is unrefined, which is why it still contains properties that keep it healthy. Oleic acid is the healthy ingredient that is good for lowering blood pressure and maintaining a healthy heart and vascular system. Olive oil can be used in many dishes as it can be a great substitute for butter or fatty salad dressings and adds a delicious flavour to fried vegetables, fish and meats.

Garlic

Garlic is an incredible vegetable with a lot of benefits to your health. It is an anti-inflammatory that has been used to treat diabetes for centuries across the globe. A clove of raw garlic has just four calories and one single gram of carbohydrates.

Strawberries

Surprisingly, strawberries are extremely low in sugar! One cup of strawberries only has 48 calories and contains 10g of carbohydrates, 3g of which are fibre. They make a wonderful, guilt-free addition to breakfast cereals, smoothies, yoghurt, or you can enjoy them chopped up with a blob of fresh cream for dessert! You can also stew fresh strawberries with a little sweetener for a low-sugar fruit compote to dollop on porridge or drizzle on drop scones.

Bad food choices for diabetics:

White rice, pasta and bread

These are all highly processed carbohydrates that have been proven to dramatically increase blood sugar levels in people with diabetes. It also decreases brain function in type 2 diabetes patients, leaving them feeling lethargic and tired. These food types are not rich in healthy fiber, which our body needs to regulate the speed with which sugar is absorbed into the bloodstream.

French fries:

Unfortunately diabetics need to stay clear of French fries, and other similar fried fast foods. Potatoes are already very high in carbohydrates on their own. An average-sized potato contains 38g of carbohydrates and only 4g of fiber. When you peel potatoes and fry them in vegetable oil, they have the potential to send your blood sugar through the roof. If you love potato and don't want to give them up completely, you can substitute with a modest amount of sweet potato, or try baby new potatoes, steamed and with the skin still on to retain the maximum amount of nutrients.

Concentrated fruit juices:

Although fruit juices are generally considered healthy, they have a similar sugar content as fizzy soda and artificially sweetened beverages. In fact, sometimes they contain even more sugar and carbohydrates and although these sugars come from a natural source, they can still leave a daiabetic's sugar levels too high. Concentrated orange juice for example contains a huge amount of fructose and high levels of fructose directly contributes to obesity, heart disease and insulin resistance.

Sugary flavoured yogurt:

Unlike greek or natural, plain, probiotic yoghurt, flavored yoghurts are packed with hidden sugars and carbohydrates. Sadly, even frozen yoghurts that have claims of being healthier than ice cream still contain the same amount of sugar, or even more, to compensate for the lack of fat.

Sweetened breakfast cereals

The majority of cereals on our supermarket shelves contain considerably more carbohydrates than people are led to believe. Despite the health claims on the boxes, even "healthy breakfast cereals" are not considered a good choice, especially for individuals with diabetes. The combination of processed grains, added sugar and dried food is a disastrous combination for people struggling to control their blood sugar levels.

Dried fruit

Although fruit is usually thought to be a healthy snack option, dried fruit comes with a lot more risk factors for hose with diabetes. Although it is undeniable that all fruit is a great source of vitamins, minerals and potassium, once the liquid is evaporated from the fruit it be comes much easier to over indulge and consume a lot more sugar than intended. For example, a cup of raisins contains more than three times as many carbs as a cup of grapes.

Maple syrup and honey

In this day of age it is fashionable to try and consume natural, less-refined sugars, such as honey and maple syrup. Unfortunately for diabetics, this "healthy" reputation is (again) not accurate. Weight for weight, these natural sugars often actually contain more sugar than your standard refined white sugar and should therefore be similarly avoided. If you are craving something sweet, it is better to reach for a sweetener instead and there are many natural sweeteners on the market, whether it's for baking or your morning coffee.

Packed snacks and confectionery

With a fast-paced modern lifestyle, it's all too easy to reach for a snack or chocolate bar for a quick and easy afternoon boost. Sadly, despite new regulations in recent years, these types of snacks are still packed with unhealthy saturated fat, sugar and carbohydrates. Although understandably difficult, diabetics are recommended to try and limit their intake of these foods and make healthier choices, such as nuts, fruits and wholegrain cereal bars.

Alcohol

Beer, wine and some spirits are deceptively high in sugars and carbohydrates. It is recommended that diabetics limit their alcohol intake to two drinks a day for men and just one drink a day for women. For those individuals who don't want to give up drinking entirely, it is suggested you switch to diet sodas, dry wine, and white grain spirits, such as vodka and gin. Beer, ale, and stout generally contain very high levels of carbohydrates, but in recent years breweries have started to produce low carb beer as well to address this problem. When it comes to diabetics and alcohol, moderation and self discipline are key.

Flavored coffee drinks

While coffee is generally considered to be a fairly healthy beverage and a great way to get a boost in the morning without sugar, the same cannot be said about flavoured coffees from your local coffee shop. These new flavored coffees we buy from Starbucks and the like should be considered more of a liquid desert, rather than a healthy morning beverage. The sugary syrups used to add the flavor, in combination with the sweetened cream and different sauces, all dramatically contribute to raised blood sugar levels and increased carbohydrate intake. Although delicious, it is highly recommended that diabetics stay clear of these coffees and stick to coffees like espressos and cappuccinos. Even if you are on a healthy meal plan, the addition of these types of beverage could hinder your weight loss.

Healthy food preparation methods

Here are a few healthy cooking techniques to minimise saturated fats in your diet, and retain the most nutrients in your food.

Steaming vegetables vs boiling vegetables:

Gently steaming vegetables is a much better way of preserving the natural vitamins and minerals in your food. This quick and simple method of cooking uses minimal water and it is easy to tell when the vegetables are ready to eat! Boiling vegetables on the other hand dilutes and strips many of the nutrients from the food, leeching them into the water. Unless you're using the boiling water to make stock, soup, or gravy, it's recommended that you always steam your vegetables.

Oven baking vs deep frying

Oven baking your chips or wedges uses considerably less oil than deep frying, and offers very similar results! We recommend chopping your potatoes thinly and brushing or tossing them lightly with olive oil, seasoning and then baking them in a hot oven for 30 to 40 minutes! While deep frying is quicker and more traditional, it uses 10 times more oil, which is not only wasteful, but also means your food instantly gains more calories. Bad trans fats, such as palm or vegetable oil have also been linked to heart disease, weight gain and cancer, so it is advisable to avoid deep drying whenever possible and stick to oven baking.

Making your own sauces vs shop bought sauces.

While they are more convenient, many shop bought sauces are jam packed with added sugar, salt, flavouring, preservatives, and carbohydrates, which are a real setback for many diabetics looking to make healthier food choices. We recommend learning a few simple sauce recipes at home and experimenting with different vegetables, seasonings and herbs. Not only is making your own sauce cheaper, but it also allows you full control over what goes into your food and dramatically lowers your calorie intake.

Keep reading to discover a selection of specially designed diabetic meals to help inspire your weight loss journey. Following the recipes will be a 10 day weight loss journal with a full meal plan for each day for you to follow. Stay safe, stay healthy and enjoy!

RECIPES

Breakfast

Delicious 5 minute tomato avocado toast

Cooking time: 5 minutes / Servings:1

CALORIES: 311 / NET CARBS: 16 G / FIBRE: 8 G / FAT: 7 G / PROTEIN: 8 G / SUGAR: 3 G /

This is a fresh and delicious idea for every diabetic! A slice of crisp sourdough covered with thick slices of tomatoes, avocado, a bit of mustard and a generous portion of melted cheese on top!

INGREDIENTS:

- 1 slice of sourdough bread

- 1 tbsp of mustard

- 2 slices of tomato

- ½ avocado smashed

- 1 slice of cheddar cheese/mozzarella

- Fresh basil optional

PREPARATION:

1. Lightly toast the bread in a toaster or an oven.

2. Spread mustard on the toasted bread.

3. Add avocado, slices of tomatoes and the cheese on top.

4. Put it under the grill/broiler until the cheese is melted.

5. Top with fresh basil.

Lean turkey bacon egg muffins

Prep time: 10 min / Cooking time: 25 min / Servings: 12

CALORIES: 88 / NET CARBS: 1.5 G / FIBRE: 0.5 G / FAT: 4.3 G / PROTEIN: 10.8 G /

This is an all-time favorite and a meal that is easy to prepare. It tastes amazing and the beauty of it is that you can easily prepare more and store it for a quick breakfast bite the next morning! These delicious and healthy turkey bacon muffins are a healthy way to start your day. Turkey, eggs and vegetables of your choice - what is there not to love?

INGREDIENTS:

- 12 slices of high quality, lean turkey bacon

- 570 g // 20 oz of egg whites

- 3 small eggs

- 20 g // 2.5 oz of lean turkey ham

- 20 g // 2.5 oz of red pepper (or yellow or green - it's up to you)

- 57 g // 2 oz of chopped spinach

- ◆ 85 g // 3 oz of yellow onion

- ◆ 1 clove of garlic

- ◆ Half a jalapeno pepper

- ◆ 1.5 tsp of salt

- ◆ 1.5 tsp of pepper

PREPARATION:

1. Preheat the oven at175 degrees C (350 F).

2. Lightly oil a 12 hole muffin pan with a little cooking spray or olive oil.

3. Using one slice of turkey bacon per hole, wrap the slice around the inside of each muffin form.

4. Place a small handful of spinach at the bottom of each.

5. In a blender, mince together the onions, jalapeno and garlic until they're very finely chopped.

6. Using a little oil in a frying pan add your chopped vegetables, garlic, onion and jalapeno mix and gently fry for a few minutes until the onions are see-through.

7. Take the veggie mix off the stove and divide it between the 12 muffin holes (placing on top of the spinach).

8. Dice up the ham and bell pepper and divide between the muffin holes.

9. Whisk together the egg whites, whole eggs, plus the salt and pepper.

10. Using a ladle or a big spoon, divide the egg mixture between each muffin ring.

11. Cook in your preheated oven for approximately 25 minutes.

Chia seed banana smoothie

Prep time: 5 min / Cooking time: 1 min / Servings: 1

CALORIES: 304 / NET CARBS: 47 G / FIBRE: 8 G / FAT: 9 G / PROTEIN: 13 G / SUGAR: 16 G /

This healthy smoothie is just perfect if you are having a busy morning and don't really have the time to cook. It is packed with lots of diabetic-friendly fiber and one of the magic ingredients, cinnamon. Once you've tasted this smoothie, we're sure it will become one of your go-to treats.

INGREDIENTS:

- ◆ 1 frozen banana
- ◆ 250 ml //1 cup of milk
- ◆ 1 tbsp of natural greek yogurt
- ◆ 1 tbsp of chia seeds
- ◆ ½ tsp of cinnamon

PREPARATION:

1. Dice your frozen banana roughly with a sharp knife. Take care as the frozen banana might be quite hard.

2. Place the ingredients in a blender and blend on high for one minute or until you are happy with the consistency.

3. Pour, serve, and enjoy!

4. If you have a sweet tooth, you can pour a teaspoon of honey into the mixture, but be cautious of the additional sugar.

Low Sugar Superfood Granola

Prep time: 5 min / Cooking time: 20 min / Servings: 16 cups / Serving size: ½ cup

CALORIES: 234 / NET CARBS: 27.5 G / FIBRE: 3.4 G / FAT: 11.8 G / PROTEIN: 3.5 G /

This granola makes a great alternative to the super sugary shop-bought versions. We love making this granola in bulk on the weekend and storing it in a tupperware container for the rest of the week. It's also really easy to adjust the flavour and crunch, depending on your personal taste.

INGREDIENTS:

- 4 cups of whole oats

- 1.5 cups of raw pecan nuts

- ½ cup of pumpkin seeds

- 1 tsp of sea salt

- ½ tsp of cinnamon

- ½ cup of coconut or olive oil

- ½ cup of maple syrup or honey

- 1 tsp of vanilla extract

- ♦ ⅔ cup of dried fruit, chopped into small pieces (dates work really well)

- ♦ Optional additions - ½ cup of coconut flakes

PREPARATION:

1. Preheat the oven at 175 degrees C (350 F).

2. Use parchment paper to line a large baking tray.

3. In a large mixing pan, combine the oats, nuts, seeds, sea salt, cinnamon and coconut flakes.

4. Pour in the oil, maple syrup and/or honey and vanilla.

5. Mix well, ensuring everything is lightly coated in liquid.

6. Spoon the granola mixture onto your baking pan and use a large spatula to spread it into an even, thin layer.

7. Bake in your oven for about 25 minutes. Stir half-way.

8. Your granola should come out lightly golden and will crisp up further as it cools down.

9. Let it cool completely for at least 45 minutes.

10. Top up with dried fruit and break the granola into pieces with your fingers, stirring it around until it becomes loose.

11. Store your granola in an airtight Tupperware for up to 14 days.

12. Alternatively, you can freeze your granola in ziplock bags for up to 3 months.

Pumpkin pancakes with a twist

Prep time: 5 min / Cooking time: 10 min / Servings: 1

CALORIES: 182 / NET CARBS: 16.1 G / FIBRE: 2.8 G / FAT: 1.3 G / PROTEIN: 22.5 G / SUGAR: 1.5 G /

These pancakes are a delicious surprise and one can hardly believe that something that tastes so good can be healthy for you! You can puree the pumpkins on your own, but if you are too busy, don't be afraid to use the canned version as it will still satisfy your taste buds! A sprinkle of Stevia to substitute sugar, and voila.

INGREDIENTS:

- ♦ 20 g // 0.7 oz of oats
- ♦ 92 g // 3.2 oz of egg whites
- ♦ 28 g // 1 oz of pumpkin puree
- ♦ Cooking spray
- ♦ 2 tsp of Stevia
- ♦ ½ tsp of cinnamon
- ♦ Optional: sugar free syrup and apple

PREPARATION:

1. Blend all of the ingredients, bar the cooking spray, until it becomes smooth.

2. Spray the cooking spray on the bottom of a small pan and put it over a medium heat.

3. Pour about ⅓ of the batter on the cooking oil and spread it around the pan evenly.

4. Before flipping it, let it cook until you see the edges going a little bit brown, then cook it for about two minutes on the other side.

5. Put it on a plate and cook the other two pancakes in the same way.

6. When you are done, serve them up with syrup, a few pieces of apple and a sprinkle of Stevia.

Delicious breakfast bowl with cottage cheese

Prep time: 10 min / Cooking time: 10 min / Servings: 1

CALORIES: 266 / NET CARBS: 18.9 G / FIBRE: 5.5 G / FAT: 14.5 G / PROTEIN: 17.7 G / SUGAR: 11.6 G /

This is another breakfast dish that is so tasty, it's really hard to believe it can be healthy as well! With the one we made, we used berries, hazelnuts and coconut, but the beauty of this recipe is that you can use whatever you want! You can use all types of nuts and seeds and let your body thank you for a beautiful start to the day!

INGREDIENTS:

- ◆ 1 cup of low fat cottage cheese

- ◆ ¼ cup of blackberries

- ◆ ¼ cup of pomegranate

- ◆ 15 g // ½ oz of coconut flakes (unsweetened)

- ◆ 30 g // 1 oz of hazelnuts

PREPARATION:

1. Use a small personal blender or a food processor and pulsate the cottage cheese until it becomes smooth. This usually takes around two or three minutes.

2. Prepare the toppings (you can toast the hazelnut in a skillet for about two minutes if you desire).

3. Serve immediately or chill for up to 24 hours.

Easy tomato, herb and cheese omelet

Prep time: 2 min / Cooking time: 8min / Servings: 1

CALORIES: 350 / NET CARBS: 1.2 G / FIBRE: 3.2 G - / FAT: 25.5 G / PROTEIN: 20.5 G /

They say preparing a perfect omelet is an art form. There are several tricks and this recipe will teach you all you need to know. The magic lies in cooking the egg for just the right amount of time, as well as at the right temperature. With enough olive oil you will save the egg from sticking to the pan. Add some vegetables of your choice, a few herbs and some cheese and you will leave your house happy and satisfied in the morning.

INGREDIENTS:

- ♦ 2 eggs
- ♦ 2 tbsp of olive oil
- ♦ ½ cup of cherry tomatoes
- ♦ ½ cup of fresh basil
- ♦ ¼ cup of cheddar cheese

PREPARATION:

1. Chop your cherry tomatoes into small pieces.

2. Add a little olive oil into your pan and preheat it on the stove.

3. Gently fry the tomatoes for 2 minutes.

4. When they start getting soft, take them off the stove and allow to cool.

5. Give your pan a wipe with a piece of a clean kitchen paper.

6. Whisk the eggs in a bowl with a fork, and add some salt and pepper.

7. Return the pan to the heat and add the remaining oil.

8. Carefully pour the egg mixture into the hot oil.

9. The egg mixture should start to bubble and solidify around the edges.

10. Turn the temperature down and add your fried tomatoes and fresh basil leaves and a sprinkling of cheese to one half of the omelet.

11. Gently cook until your egg mixture is crisping up around the edges and the cheese has melted slightly.

12. Gently wiggle the pan back and forth. Your omelet should be moving around freely and not sticking to the pan.

13. Using a spatula, fold the side of the omelet with no filling over.

14. The melted cheese should stick and hold the omelet neatly together.

15. Serve your omelet with a few more basil leaves on top for better presentation.

Main dishes

Garlic artichoke stuffed chicken breast

Prep time: 5 min / Cooking time: 20 min / Servings: 1

CALORIES: 262 / NET CARBS: 8.5 G / FIBRE: 2.4 G / FAT: 4.1 G / PROTEIN: 46 G /

This is an amazing option for anyone, not just diabetics! We're confident that your whole family will really enjoy this meal and request it time and time again. It's very easy to prepare, so it's a perfect weeknight lunch when you've had a busy day. Chicken stuffed with cheese, garlic, basil, tomato and artichoke, sure to satisfy even the most demanding taste buds.

INGREDIENTS:

- ◆ 1 chicken breast (medium size)

- ◆ 1 artichoke heart from a can (or fresh if you have it)

- ◆ 30g // 1 oz of mozzarella (low fat)

- ◆ 1.5 tsp of chopped sundried tomatoes

- ◆ 1 clove of garlic

- ◆ 6 big basil leaves

- ♦ ¼ tsp of curry powder

- ♦ ¼ tsp of red paprika

- ♦ ⅕ tsp of pepper

PREPARATION:

1. First, preheat the oven to 365 F (185 C).

2. Cut the chicken breast lengthwise to create a pocket for the filling.

3. Prepare the filling by chopping up the tomato, artichoke, mozzarella, basil and garlic, and combine it all together.

4. Stuff the mixture in the pocket of the chicken breast. You can use toothpicks to keep the stuffing in place.

5. Place it on a baking sheet (aluminum foil will do as well) and season with the curry powder, paprika and pepper.

6. Bake for approximately 20 minutes until the juices are running clear (this might take a bit longer if your chicken breast is large).

7. Remove from the oven, take out the toothpicks and you're ready to serve up your delicious lunch!

Chicken and egg salad

Prep time: 5 min / Cooking time: 20 minutes / Servings: 4

CALORIES: 175 / NET CARBS: 1.5 G / FIBRE: 0.8 G / FAT: 5.4 G / PROTEIN: 30.4 G /

This is an easy and healthy dinner recipe for those who like to eat lightly before going to bed. It's perfect for meal prepping too, as you can whip up a batch and leave it in your refrigerator until you want it. It is also a very affordable meal! Delicious cooked chicken with curry powder, eggs and mayo. Serve on multi-grain bread and voila!

INGREDIENTS:

- ◆ 2 chicken breasts (cooked)

- ◆ 3 eggs (hard boiled)

- ◆ 2 tbsp of low fat mayo

- ◆ 1 tbsp of curry powder

- ◆ Chives or basil (optional)

- ◆ Salt

PREPARATION:

1. First, bake the chicken breast in the oven at365 F (185 C) for around 20 minutes.

2. Hard boil the eggs (usually around 8 minutes).

3. Mix the mayo with the curry powder (feel free to add more).

4. Combine everything in a bowl and mix it.

5. Allow the mixture to chill in the fridge (10 minutes minimum, but longer if possible).

6. Add salt and chives or basil and serve on multi-grain bread or with celery sticks if you really want to go carb-free!

Sweet potato frittata

Prep time: 10 min / Cooking time: 50 min / Servings: 4

CALORIES: 270 / NET CARBS: 21 G / FIBRE: 2 G / FAT: 12 G / PROTEIN: 18 G / SUGAR: 5 G

You can never go wrong with a frittata. And who could ever resist a slice of this delicious dish when coming home from work or school in the afternoon? It tastes delicious hot or cold and can be eaten for lunch with a side salad. Heaven...

INGREDIENTS:

- 1 large sweet potato

- 114 g // 4 oz of diced ham

- 6 eggs

- 2 tbsp of greek yogurt

- ½ tsp of black pepper

- ½ tsp of sea salt

- ½ cup of grated cheddar cheese

PREPARATION:

1. Peel and finely dice the sweet potato.

2. Gently fry the sweet potato with a teaspoon of olive oil until soft.

3. Preheat the oven at 175 degrees C (350 F).

4. Line and grease a medium sized baking pan.

5. Beat together eggs, ham, seasoning and yogurt.

6. Stir in the cubes of sweet potato and pour mixture into the lined baking pan.

7. Sprinkle cheese on top if desired and bake for around 50 minutes until it all looks cooked.

Healthy salmon with spring vegetables

Cooking time: 25 min / Servings: 4

CALORIES: 230 / NET CARBS: 3 G / FIBRE: 1 G / FAT: 2.5 G / PROTEIN: 23 G /

Salmon is one of the healthiest things you can eat as a diabetic. Just look at the nutritional value! This is so easy to make and will satisfy the deepest cravings for fish. The flavor of lemon and pepper really give it a special something that will make you want to eat it everyday!

INGREDIENTS:

♦ 2 tbsp of olive oil

♦ 2 tbsp of fresh basil

♦ 1 tsp of fresh grated lemon peel

♦ 270 g // 8 oz of asparagus (fresh spears)

♦ 1 bell pepper (colour optional)

♦ 2 tsp of extra-virgin olive oil

♦ ½ tsp of pepper

- ♦ ½ tsp of pepper-lemon seasoning

- ♦ ½ tsp of garlic salt

- ♦ 1 whole salmon fillet (500 g)

PREPARATION:

1. Preheat the contact grill (medium sized, heat closed) for about 5 minutes.

2. In a small bowl Mix the basil, lemon peel and olive oil.

3. Season the bell pepper and asparagus with 1 tsp of oil and ¼ tsp of pepper, garlic salt and lemon pepper.

4. When the grill is heated enough, put the vegetables on the grill and cook them covered for about four to five minutes or until the vegetables are tender.

5. Cut the salmon into four symmetrical pieces. Brush them with oil and then season with the remaining salt and pepper. Place them on the grill, skin side down.

6. Close the grill and cook the salmon for four to five minutes, until you can pierce the fish easily with a fork.

7. Serve it with the vegetables and the pre-prepared virgin olive oil mix.

Chicken soup with coconut

Prep time: 20 min / Cooking time: 30 min / Servings: 6

CALORIES: 231 / NET CARBS: 10 G / FIBRE: 1.7 G / FAT: 12.8 G / PROTEIN: 17 G / SUGAR: 5 G

This dish is simply amazing. Filled with flavor, different veggies and lean chicken breast it's also healthy and above all, filling! It will warm your belly and keep you satisfied for hours. A perfect solution for lunch or dinner. And if you have leftovers you can just store them in the refrigerator as this dish reheats very well.

INGREDIENTS:

- ♦ 1 tbsp of coconut oil

- ♦ 2 minced garlic cloves

- ♦ 1 small piece of ginger (peeled and grated)

- ♦ One small onion (sliced in thin half moons)

- ♦ 1 diced medium courgette/zucchini

- 500 g // 1 lb of sliced chicken breast

- 340 g // 0.75 lb of cubed pumpkin (around 1 cm // ½ inch pieces)

- 1 red bell pepper (sliced thinly)

- 1 small sliced chilli

- 1 can of light coconut milk (around 450 ml // 14 oz)

- 2 cups of chicken broth

- 1 slice of lime

- 1 handful of coriander // cilantro leaves (optional)

- Salt and pepper

PREPARATION:

1. Salt and pepper your chicken.

2. Heat the oil in a large pan and fry the chicken breast for around four or five minutes, or until it gets a nice white color.

3. Add the ginger, garlic and onion and stir-fry for an extra two or three minutes

4. Stir in the pumpkin and courgette/zucchini.

5. Then add all of the remaining ingredients, the bell pepper, chilli, chicken broth, lime juice and coconut milk, and stir it well.

6. Bring it to a boil, lower the heat and let it cook for around 20 minutes (or until the pumpkin is soft).

7. Add some salt and pepper to suit your taste, top with coriander/cilantro (if you like it) and serve.

Healthy colorful beef fajitas

Prep time: 5 min / Cooking time: 10 min / Servings: 4

CALORIES: 336 / NET CARBS: 10.5 G / FIBRE: 4.5 G / FAT: 16.7 G / PROTEIN: 30.4 G / SUGAR: 4.6 G /

This colourful fajita recipe is always a winner, perfect for summer days. A healthy, easy recipe that takes less than 20 minutes to prepare and it's filled with protein, good veggie carbs and healthy fat. Perfect for weeknight dinners!

INGREDIENTS:

- ◆ 450 g // 1 lb of stir-fry beef strips

- ◆ 1 red and 1 yellow bell pepper (deseeded, sliced into 0.5 cm // ¼ inch long thick stripes)

- ◆ 1 red onion (sliced)

- ◆ ½ tsp of cumin

- ◆ ½ tsp of chilli powder

- ◆ A splash of oil

- ◆ 1 avocado

- Lime juice (from half a lime)

- Salt and pepper

- Freshly chopped coriander // cilantro

PREPARATION:

1. Heat a frying pan over medium heat.

2. Heat the oil and add the beef stir-fry in three separate batches.

3. Salt and pepper each batch in the pan (add a generous amount).

4. Cook for around 1 minute per side (until the color is right) and set aside.

5. Once all three batches of the beef is cooked, keep the meat juice in the pan and add the bell pepper and onions. Add the chilli powder and cumin and then stir-fry until it reaches the level of softness you prefer.

6. Transfer everything to a plate, drizzle it with fresh lemon juice, sprinkle with the coriander/cilantro and add sliced avocado.

Meatballs with turkey

Prep time: 15 min / Cooking time: 25 min / Servings: 5

CALORIES: 183 / NET CARBS: 12 G / FIBRE: 3 G / FAT: 2.5 G / PROTEIN: 30.8 G / SUGAR: 2.9 G /

This meal is an absolute favorite in many households with healthy eating habits. It doesn't contain any breadcrumbs, which means a lower level of carbs, but you won't miss them! It's juicy, filled with turkey and vegetables and ready in just 40 minutes- what more can we ask for? The meatballs can also be stored in an airtight container for three or four days in the fridge, or even longer if you like to prep your food and freeze it.

INGREDIENTS:

- ◆ 270 g // 10 oz ground turkey

- ◆ ¼ cup of oats

- ◆ 2 egg whites

- ◆ 100 g // 3.5 oz of spinach (fresh or frozen, chopped)

- ◆ 3 cloves of garlic (chopped finely)

- ◆ 2 celery sticks (chopped finely)

- ½ of onion (chopped finely)

- ½ cup of parsley (chopped)

- ½ of green bell pepper (deseeded and chopped)

- 1 tsp of mustard powder

- 1 tsp of thyme

- ½ tsp of cumin

- ½ tsp of chipotle pepper

- ½ tsp of turmeric

- 1 tsp of salt

- 1 pinch of pepper

PREPARATION:

1. First, preheat the oven to 365 F (185 C).

2. Mix the garlic, onion and celery in a large mixing bowl, then add the egg whites, turkey, oats and spices and mix until it's smooth.

3. Add the spinach, bell pepper and parsley and mix until it's well combined.

4. Line a baking sheet with parchment paper.

5. With the mixture make 15 balls, approximately the size of golf balls, and put them on the baking sheet.

6. Bake the meatballs for around 25 minutes - until they are cooked through.

Quick smoked salmon wrap with cream cheese

Prep time: 10 min / Servings: 1

CALORIES: 291 / NET CARBS: 17.9 G / FIBRE: 6.6 G / FAT: 15.3 G / PROTEIN: 23.7 G / SUGAR: 3 G

These wraps are absolutely perfect when you don't really have enough time to cook for lunch or dinner. Just mix the ingredients and wrap them and get ready to eat. Instead of a traditional bagel, we use a low-carb tortilla to reduce the carbs and make this meal even healthier. They are tasty, healthy, easy and they might just become your favorite go-to lunch or dinner!

INGREDIENTS:

- 57 g // 2 oz of smoked salmon

- 1 tbsp of low fat cream cheese

- 120 cm // 8 inch low carb flour tortilla

- 75 g // ¼ oz of red onion (finely sliced)

- 1 handful of rocket // arugula

- ½ tsp of fresh chopped basil (or dried)

♦ Salt and pepper

PREPARATION:

1. Mix the cream cheese, basil and pepper.

2. Warm up the tortilla in the oven or microwave and to keep it from drying out, use two pieces of moist paper towel and warm the tortilla in between them.

3. Spread the cream cheese mixture onto the tortilla.

4. Add the salmon, onion and rocket/arugula.

5. Roll up the tortilla and you are done!

Chicken tenders baked with mustard

Prep time: 5 min / Cooking time: 20 min / Servings: 4

CALORIES: 195 / NET CARBS: 3.6 G / FIBRE: 1.4 G / FAT: 4.5 G / PROTEIN: 28.5 G / SUGAR: 2 G

This is a great recipe to turn to when you feel like you are out of ideas for a healthy meal. Chicken tenders - it doesn't get more basic than that! The mustard gives it a little kick, changing an otherwise plain dish into something a bit more spicy and adventurous. The flavor is not too strong or spicy, however, so even the kids will enjoy it. Chicken is a great source of protein for any diabetic and the mustard sauce is a breeze to prepare. You can serve it as it is or with a side salad.

INGREDIENTS:

- ♦ 450 g // 1 lb of chicken tenders
- ♦ 2 ½ tbsp of chopped fresh tarragon
- ♦ ½ of cup of whole grain mustard
- ♦ 1 tbsp of lemon juice
- ♦ 1 clove of minced garlic
- ♦ ½ tsp of pepper

- ¼ tsp of salt
- ½ tsp of paprika
- Tarragon for garnish

PREPARATION:

1. First, preheat the oven to 425 F(220 C).
2. Mix together the pepper, salt, paprika, lemon juice, garlic, tarragon and mustard.
3. Add the chicken to the mix making sure that each piece of chicken is covered with the mustard sauce.
4. Put the chicken into a large baking dish and cover it in the oven.
5. Bake until the chicken is cooked through (around 15 to 20 minutes).

Snacks & Desserts

Low carb sugar free peanut butter cookies

Prep time: 5 min / Cooking time: 15 min / Servings: 12

CALORIES: 140 / NET CARBS: 4 G / FIBRE: 1.3 G / FAT: 10.3 G / PROTEIN: 5.8 G / SUGAR: 0 G

These cookies are a great way to satisfy your sweet tooth with a healthy snack. They do not contain any sugar and they are low on carbohydrates, so they are a perfect choice for weight loss and for diabetics. Only five ingredients that all come together in one bowl, so they are extremely easy to make.

INGREDIENTS:

- 1 cup of peanut butter with no added sugar and no chunks
- 1 egg
- ⅔ cup of erythritol (a sugar substitute)
- ½ tsp of vanilla essence
- ½ tsp of baking soda

PREPARATION:

1. First, preheat the oven to 350 F (180 C).

2. Use non-stick baking paper to line a cooking tray.

3. Powder the erythritol in a blender.

4. Stir all of the ingredients until smooth.

5. Take 2 tablespoons of dough for each cookie and roll it in your fingers to create a ball. Using all of the dough, you should get between 12 and 14 cookies. Place the balls on the cooking tray.

6. With a fork, flatten the balls, so you get a double-cross pattern on each cookie.

7. Bake for around 12 to 15 minutes and then take them out and allow to cool for around 40 minutes.

Low carb cheesecake heaven

Prep time: 10 min / Cooking time: 50 min / Servings: 2

CALORIES: 165 / NET CARBS: 6 G / FIBRE: 0 G / FAT: 0.6 G / PROTEIN: 32 G / SUGAR:3.5 G

It is hard to describe just how flavourful and mouth-watering this cheesecake is. Let us assure you that you're not missing out on delicious desserts simply because you are trying to be healthy. This cheesecake can compete with any other fatty cheesecake you can find! This is a gem with almost no fat, carbs or calories. Give it a try and you won't regret it.

INGREDIENTS:

- ♦ 241 g // 8.5 oz of low fat cottage cheese

- ♦ 1 tsp of vanilla extract

- ♦ 1 scoop of vanilla protein powder

- ♦ 1 tsp of sweetener (Stevia or others)

- ♦ 2 egg whites

- ♦ Water

♦ 1 serving of sugar-free jelly //
jello (the flavour is up to you)

PREPARATION:

1. First, preheat the oven to 325 F (160 C).

2. Prepare the jelly/jello (instructions are on the box) and put it in the freezer.

3. Blend the egg whites and the cottage cheese until you get a smooth mixture.

4. Add the protein powder, vanilla extract and your sweetener and whisk them all together.

5. Put the batter in a small pan(a non-stick pan is the best),place it in the oven and bake for about 25 minutes.

6. Turn off the oven, but wait until the oven cools down before removing the cheesecake. Once the oven is cool, take it out.

7. Pour the jelly/jello all over the cheesecake.

8. Put it in a fridge and let it cool and set for about 10 to 12 hours before taking a slice!

Deviled eggs with horseradish

Prep time: 10 min / Cooking time: 10 min / Servings: 12 / 2 per serving

CALORIES: 146 / NET CARBS: 1 G / CHOLESTEROL: 215 MG / FAT: 13 G / SUGAR: 1 G

Who in this world doesn't like tangy deviled eggs? This is a very appealing combination, perhaps a bit more bold than others, but the flavors really come together in a tasty and appetizing combination. It takes 30 minutes to prepare, but it's worth every minute. Suitable for your own snacking needs or for a party full of people. No matter why you are preparing them, one thing is certain - they will be devoured down to the last bite.

INGREDIENTS:

- 6 eggs
- 2 tbsp of very thinly chopped horseradish
- ¼ cup of low fat mayo
- 1 pinch of pepper
- 3/4 tsp of salt
- ¼ tsp of dill weed

- ◆ 1 pinch of paprika

- ◆ 1 tsp of ground mustard

PREPARATION:

1. Fill a saucepan with cold water. Place the eggs at the bottom ensuring that they are covered with water (at least 2.5 cm // 1 inch).

2. Bring the water to a boil and add a half a teaspoon of salt to make the eggs easier to peel once cooked.

3. Cover, turn the heat off and let the pan sit on the hot stove for around 10 to 12 minutes. Strain the water and run cold water over the eggs, so that they stop cooking and cool.

4. Peel the eggs and cut them in half lengthwise. Remove the egg yolks and put the egg whites aside.

5. In a big mixing bowl combine the egg yolks, dill, mustard, mayo, salt, pepper, and horseradish. Mix well.

6. Use a spoon to return the mixture into the egg whites.

7. Refrigerate for 10 to 20 minutes, sprinkle with paprika and serve.

Healthy low carb chicken nuggets

Prep time: 15 min / Cooking time: 25 min / Servings: 2

CALORIES: 311 / NET CARBS: 3.1 G / FIBRE: 1.5 G / FAT: 24 G / PROTEIN: 25 G / SUGAR:0.5 G

It is hard to believe that such an easy recipe could be so healthy and such a family favorite. It's a grain-free recipe with merely six ingredients. We use almond flour in this recipe, but in case you have an allergy, you can easily substitute it with coconut flour! There are many low carb condiments as dipping sauce as well - from mustard to avocado oil or low fat mayo, whatever your heart desires.

INGREDIENTS:

- ♦ 2 skinless and boneless chicken breasts
- ♦ ½ cup of almond or coconut flour
- ♦ 1 tbsp of Italian seasoning
- ♦ 2 tbsp of extra virgin olive oil
- ♦ ½ tsp of salt
- ♦ ½ tsp of pepper

PREPARATION:

1. First, preheat the oven to 400 F (200 C) and put parchment paper on your baking sheet.

2. Stir the salt, pepper, almond flour and Italian seasoning in a bowl until the mixture is smooth.

3. Cut the chicken into 2.5 cm (1 inch) thick pieces and remove the fat, then spray it with olive oil.

4. Put the chicken pieces in the bowl and toss them with the flour mixture. Put the pieces on the baking sheet.

5. First, bake it for 20 minutes. Then put the grill/broiler on and leave the chicken pieces under the heat for a couple of minutes, so they become crispy.

6. Serve with a condiment for dipping.

Skinny chocolate chip cookies

Prep time: 5 min / Cooking time: 15 min / Servings: 8

CALORIES: 165 / NET CARBS: 9.5 G / FIBRE: 2.4 G / FAT: 14.4 G / PROTEIN: 3.3 G / SUGAR: 0.4 G

Delicious, easy and grain-free. What more can you ask for from a cookie? They are a great treat, even for the most demanding taste buds. A guilt-free dessert with only 165 calories per cookie, with no added sugar and no carbs. They will satisfy your chocolate cravings and keep you on a healthy path. You don't believe us? Try this recipe out and you will never have a sugary cookie again.

INGREDIENTS:

- 4 tbsp of butter

- 3 tbsp of ground flax meal

- ½ cup of erythritol (or any granulated sweetener you like)

- 3 tbsp of water

- 1 ½ cup of almond flour

- ½ of cup of chocolate chips (you have to use the sugar-free kind)

- ◆ 1 tsp of baking soda

- ◆ 1 pinch of salt

PREPARATION:

1. First, preheat the oven to 325 F (160 C). Line your baking tray with parchment paper.

2. Powder the erythritol in a blender.

3. Mix the butter and the sweetener until you get a smooth consistency and the sweetener is dissolved.

4. Add the almond flour, baking soda, water and ground flax until all of the ingredients are well combined.

5. Add the chocolate chips until they are evenly distributed in the dough.

6. Form the dough into cookie shapes (about 1 tbsp at a time) and put them on the baking tray. You should have enough dough for about 8 cookies.

7. Bake them for around 15 to 20 minutes until golden brown.

8. Remove them from the oven and let them cool for 10 minutes, then transfer them on a rack and let them cool for another 10 minutes. Enjoy!

The 10 Day Weight Loss Journal

DAY 1

Breakfast: Prep time:5 minutes / Cooking time: 10 min / Serves: 2

CALORIES: 321 / NET CARBS: 16.7 G / FIBRE: 11 G / PROTEIN: 11.8 G / SUGAR: 2.1 G /

LOW CARB OATMEAL

This fat-free, low-carb oatmeal is delicious and an excellent choice for anyone who is prepared to put a little time and effort into their breakfast and reap the rewards! A great choice for fueling up before a busy day at work or school and it's ready in only 15 minutes. It tastes like the real thing, even though it's oat free.

INGREDIENTS:

- ◆ 1/2 cup of almond flour

- ◆ 4 tbsp of coconut flour

- ◆ 2 tbsp of chia seeds

- ◆ 1 tsp of ground cinnamon

- ◆ 10 – 15 drops of liquid Stevia (or other sweetener)

- ◆ 1 1/2 cup of unsweetened almond milk

♦ 1 tsp of vanilla extract

♦ salt to taste

PREPARATION:

1. In a mixing bowl whisk together the almond and coconut flour, chia seeds, flax seed powder and cinnamon until the mixture is smooth.

2. Use a medium sized pot and add the dry ingredients over a medium heat.

3. Then add the almond milk, sweetener and vanilla extract.

4. Cook the oatmeal until it is warmed and starting to thicken (around three to five minutes).

5. Serve it with any healthy toppings you like!

Lunch: Chicken soup with coconut (See page 60)

Dinner: Healthy colourful beef fajitas (See page 63)

DAY 2

Breakfast: Easy tomato, herb and cheese omelette (See page 48)

Lunch: Prep time: 10 min / Serves 1

CALORIES: 310 / NET CARBS: 34 G / FIBER: 5 G / FAT: 9 G / PROTEIN: 31 G / SUGAR: 15 G /

HEALTHY DELI-STYLE TURKEY BREAST SCHOOL LUNCH

This healthy lunch is a quick and easy version of what our mothers used to pack for us when we were going to school. It's easy to make and ideal belly filler for those who are very busy or have to eat on the go. Even if you do have enough time for cooking, you can always use the extra time for some quick meditation or yoga!

INGREDIENTS:

- ◆ 1 tbsp of hummus

- ◆ 4 thin slices of cucumber

- ◆ 1 packet of Greek yogurt (57 g // 2 oz)

- ◆ 1/2 cup of sliced blueberries and strawberries

- 14 g // 1/2 oz of low fat cheddar cheese

- 1 tsp of sunflower seeds

- 1 tsp of mustard

- 1 leaf of lettuceof your choice

- 1whole grain dinner roll

- 57g // 2 oz of turkey breast (deli style)

PREPARATION:

1. Spread the mustard on the bread roll and top it up with turkey, lettuce and cheese to make a sandwich.

2. Spread a portion of the hummus on one slice of cucumber, sprinkle with sunflower seeds, and top it off with another slice of cucumber (and repeat).

3. Including the fruit and yoghurt on the side creates the perfect low fat and healthy lunch box.

Dinner: Deviled eggs with horseradish (See page 78)

DAY 3

Breakfast: Lean turkey bacon egg muffins (See page 36)

Lunch: Healthy colourful beef fajitas (See page 63)

Dinner: Prep time: 5 min / Cooking time: 20 minutes / Serves 4

CALORIES: 175 / NET CARBS: 0 / SUGAR: 0 / PROTEIN: 22 G /

BAKED FISH FILLET WITH DIJON AND THYME TOPPING

This is another easy and healthy dinner recipe for those who don't want to eat something too heavy before going to bed. It's affordable and makes for easy meal prepping - our favourite! Deliciously cooked fish with tasty toppings. Serve it with a side salad and you're winning at the healthy lifestyle game.

INGREDIENTS:

♦ Nonstick cooking spray

♦ 4 mild fish fillets (115 g // 4 oz each, rinsed)

♦ 3 tbsp of light margarine (trans fat free)

- 2 tbsp of finely chopped fresh parsley

- 1 tsp of Dijon mustard

- ¼ tsp of crumbled dried thyme

- ¼ tsp of red-hot pepper sauce

- Salt

PREPARATION:

1. First, preheat the oven to 365 F (175 C).

2. Spray a baking sheet with the cooking spray and place the fish on it.

3. Bake for 18 to 20 minutes. When cooked, the fish should flake when piercing it with a fork.

4. Stir the remaining ingredients in a bowl.

5. Spread the mixture onto the fish.

6. Serve with a side salad.

DAY 4

Breakfast: Prep time: 5 min / Cooking time: 10 min / Serves 1

CALORIES: 242 / NET CARBS: 23.9 G / FAT: 16 G / PROTEIN: 5.9 G / SUGAR: 3 G /

HEALTHY AVOCADO TOAST WITH SCRAMBLED EGGS

The souped-up edition of delicious toast with avocado. This variation comes with scrambled eggs and will help provide an energetic start to your day, no matter how tough it's going to be. Load up and get your energy levels up in the morning!

INGREDIENTS:

- ◆ 1 peeled and seeded avocado

- ◆ 1 tbsp of lime juice

- ◆ 2 tbsp of chopped coriander // cilantro

- ◆ 1/2 tsp red pepper flakes

- ◆ 2 slices of whole grain bread

- ◆ 2 scrambled eggs (you can also use fried or poached eggs)

- ◆ Salt & pepper

PREPARATION:

1. Put the two slices of bread in a toaster and wait until they are golden brown.

2. Mash the avocado and add the coriander/cilantro, lime, pepper flakes, salt and pepper and mix well.

3. Spread the mixture over the bread slices and cover with one scrambled egg each. Sprinkle with any excess red pepper flakes and enjoy!

Lunch: Quick smoked salmon wrap with cream cheese (See page 68)

Dinner: Healthy low carb chicken nuggets (See page 80)

DAY 5

Breakfast: Chia seed banana smoothie (See page 39)

Lunch: Prep time: 15 min / Cooking time: 40 min / Serves 2

CALORIES: 310 / NET CARBS: 19.5 G / FIBRE: 5 G / FAT: 6.7 G / PROTEIN: 27.2 G / SUGAR: 6.6 G

DELICIOUS LOW CARB SPINACH ROLLS

You can never go wrong with spinach (ask Popeye!). These delicious rolls are a treat for anyone that doesn't mind a vegetarian dish every now and again. The rolls only take 20 minutes to prepare and they are best served fresh, but for those of you who like to prepare food in advance - these rolls also keep very well.

INGREDIENTS:

- ◆ 455 g // 16 oz of frozen spinach leaves (you can also use fresh spinach)

- ◆ 70 g // 2.5 oz of onion (finely chopped)

- ◆ 114 g // 4 oz of cottage cheese (fat free if possible)

- ◆ 3 eggs

- ◆ 28 g // 1 oz of carrots (grated)

- ◆ ¾ of a cup of parsley (finely chopped)

- ◆ 28 g // 1 oz of mozzarella (fat free)

- ◆ 1 clove of garlic

- ◆ 1 tsp salt

- ◆ 1 tsp pepper

- ◆ ¼ tsp of chilli flakes

- ◆ 1 tsp of curry powder

- ◆ Cooking spray

PREPARATION:

1. First, preheat the oven to 400 F (200 C).
2. If using frozen spinach, thaw and then strain the water.
3. Put the two eggs, garlic, mozzarella and the spinach with half the salt and pepper into a mixing bowl.
4. Spray the parchment paper with cooking oil and place it on a baking tray before transferring the spinach and mozzarella mix onto the paper. Press it flat to about 25 - 30 cm (10 - 12 inch) and approximately 1.2 cm (½ inch) thick.
5. Bake for about 15 minutes, put aside to cool and do not turn off the oven.
6. With a skillet or a hot pan, fry the onions for a minute.
7. Add the previously chopped parsley and carrots and leave to simmer for roughly two minutes.
8. Throw in the rest of the salt and pepper, the curry powder, the chilli and the cottage cheese and stir lightly.
9. Lay out the mixture over chilled spinach. Try not to let the mixture spill over the edges as you roll up the spinach mat and filling.
10. Place the spinach rolls in the hot oven and bake it for 25 minutes.
11. Once baked, remove the tray from the oven and let the rolls cool down for five or more minutes before serving.

Dinner: Meatballs with turkey (See page 65)

DAY 6

Breakfast: Pumpkin pancakes with a twist (See page 44)

Lunch: Chicken tenders baked with mustard (See page 70)

Dinner: Prep time: 10 min / Serves 5

CALORIES: 235 / NET CARBS: 8.6 G / FIBRE: 1.7 G / FAT: 5.7 G / PROTEIN: 29 G / SUGAR: 5.2 G

DELICIOUS AND NUTRITIOUS APPLE SALAD WITH CURRY CHICKEN

This salad is one of the healthiest things you can eat as a diabetic - just look at the nutritional value! It is simple to prepare and cook and will satisfy all your cravings for curry. Contrary to some variations of this salad, this recipe is higher in protein by switching up a creamy dressing with natural yogurt and a hint of tahini. Let's eat this every day!

INGREDIENTS:

♦ 450 g // 1 lb of diced, cooked chicken breast

♦ 2 onions (diced)

♦ 2 diced celery sticks (diced)

- ♦ 1 Granny Smith apple (finely chopped)
- ♦ 1 cup of Greek yogurt
- ♦ ½ cup of cashew nuts (chopped)
- ♦ 1 tbsp of tahini
- ♦ 1 tsp of ground cinnamon
- ♦ 4 tsp of curry powder

PREPARATION:

1. Mix the tahini, curry powder, cinnamon and yogurt in a large bowl.
2. Add the chicken, celery, onions, apples and cashews and stir.
3. Best served cold, this salad can be eaten in various ways. As a side, in a sandwich, or even with tropical fruit.

DAY 7

Breakfast: Prep time: 5 min / Serves 1

CALORIES: 350 / NET CARBS: 40 G / FAT: 15 G / PROTEIN: 21 G / SUGAR: 34 G /

AVOCADO AND BERRY SMOOTHIE

Avocado is our absolute favorite, so let's utilize it's magic as much as we can. This is an interesting and mouth-watering smoothie, but best of all it's jam-packed with vitamins - avocado, berries and Greek yoghurt delight.

INGREDIENTS:

- ♦ ½ of an avocado
- ♦ ¼ cup of blueberries
- ♦ 1 cup of strawberries
- ♦ ½ cup of low fat Greek yogurt
- ♦ ½ cup of low fat milk
- ♦ Honey (optional)

PREPARATION:

1. Combine all of the ingredients above and blend until it's smooth.

2. If you prefer your smoothies sweet, add honey to taste.

3. Serve immediately or store chilled for up to two days.

Lunch: Chicken tenders baked with mustard (See page 70)

Dinner: Garlic and artichoke stuffed chicken breast (See page 52)

DAY 8

Breakfast: Delicious 5 minute tomato avocado toast (See page 34)

Lunch: Prep time: 20 min / Cooking time: 6 hours / Serves 8

CALORIES: 271 / NET CARBS: 18 G / FIBRE: 2 G / FAT: 10 G / PROTEIN: 25 G / SUGAR: 10 G /

TENDER BEEF FRESH LETTUCE BOATS

Think tacos, but think way healthier! Replacing simple carbohydrates with a fresh leaf of lettuce makes this dish a considerably healthier option than traditional tacos. Bursting with Latin American flavours, this taco alternative is guaranteed to make your taste buds tingle.

INGREDIENTS:

- ◆ 900 g (2 lbs) of boneless chuck beef

- ◆ 2 medium sized sweet red peppers (chopped)

- ◆ 1 onion (chopped)

- ◆ 3 carrots (peeled and chopped)

- ◆ 220 g // 8 oz of unsweetened canned pineapple

- ◆ 2 tbsp of grounds sugar
- ◆ 2 tbsp of white vinegar
- ◆ ½ cup of soy sauce
  (with low sodium)
- ◆ 1 minced garlic clove
- ◆ 3 tbsp of cornstarch
- ◆ ½ tsp of black pepper
- ◆ 3 tbsp of water
- ◆ 24 romaine lettuce leaves

PREPARATION:

1. In a four litre (4-5 qts) slow cooker, combine the meat, peppers, onion and carrots.

2. Premix the vinegar, minced garlic, brown sugar, pineapple, soy sauce and black pepper and pour over the roast.

3. Slow cook for six to eight hours, until the meat is tender.

4. Remove the beef, allow to cool and shred with a couple of forks.

5. Transfer the vegetables and skimmed juices into a small pan on the stove. Once the pan is boiling, add cornstarch mixed with water. Cook until the sauce gets thick, around three to four minutes.

6. Return the vegetables, beef and thickened sauce to the slow cooker for a further 15 minutes.

7. Use your lettuce leaves as wraps for your tasty beef and veggie mix.

Dinner: Low carb cheesecake heaven (See page 76)

DAY 9

Breakfast: Sweet potato frittata (See page 56)

Lunch: Chicken and egg salad (See page 54)

Dinner: Prep time: 5 min / Cooking time: 30 min / Serves 6

CALORIES: 356 / NET CARBS: 26 G / FIBRE: 4 G / FAT: 5 G % / PROTEIN: 32 G /

CHICKEN BURGERS WITH WHOLE GRAIN BUNS AND FETA

These tasty grilled burgers are ideal for any meat lover. They are flavourful and juicy and all the ingredients create a simple, yet low-carb and low-fat chicken meal, appropriate for any occasion. So fire up that grill and let's get started!

INGREDIENTS:

- ◆ 450 g // 1 lbs of ground chicken
- ◆ 1 cup of feta (crumbled)
- ◆ ½ cup of roasted sweet red peppers (chopped)
- ◆ 1 tsp of garlic powder
- ◆ ½ tsp of Greek seasoning

- ¼ of tsp of pepper

- Lettuce leaves

- Tomato slices

- 6 whole wheat toasted burger buns

- ¼ cup of cucumber (chopped)

- ¼ cup of low fat mayo

PREPARATION:

1. Heat up the grill/broiler.

2. Stir the cucumber into the low-fat mayonnaise and put aside.

3. Mix the peppers and seasonings together and add the chicken and Feta cheese to create a firm, but sticky texture.

4. Shape six patties, approximately 1.2 cm (½ inch) in thickness.

5. Broil the patties 10 cm (4 inch) away from the heat.

6. Cook for three to four minutes.

7. Lightly toast the whole wheat buns, spread the cucumber mayo sauce and add the lettuce, tomato and patties.

DAY 10

Breakfast: Prep time: 5 min / Cooking time: 3 min / Serves: 6

CALORIES: 90 / NET CARBS: 23 G / FAT: 0.1 G / PROTEIN: 1.6 G / FIBRE: 1.7 G / SUGAR: 20.2 G /

FRUIT SALAD WITH A YOGURT GLAZE

Whenever you have fresh fruit at home, this salad is the perfect start to your day. Packed with vitamins and minerals this is as healthy as a breakfast gets. This fruit salad is tossed in a vanilla Greek yogurt dressing, which makes it feel somewhat more decadent.

INGREDIENTS:

- ◆ 425 g // 15 oz of canned mandarine oranges, drain and reserve juice
- ◆ 1 cup of strawberries (sliced)
- ◆ 1 cup of cantaloupe (in chunks)
- ◆ ½ cup of blueberries
- ◆ 1 cup of honeydew melon (in chunks)
- ◆ 2 tsp of cornstarch

- ♦ 2 tbsp of water
- ♦ ¼ cup of vanilla Greek yogurt (low-fat)
- ♦ 2 tbsp of honey

PREPARATION:

1. Mix the reserved juice, honey, cornstarch and water on medium heat for about three to four minutes or until thickened.

2. Pour the mixture out and leave it to cool before stirring in the yogurt.

3. Place all the fruit into a large bowl and pour the syrup over the top, stirring gently to create an even glaze.

4. Bon appetit!

Lunch: Meatballs with turkey (See page 65)

Dinner: Quick smoked salmon wrap with cream cheese (See page 68)

Printed in Poland
by Amazon Fulfillment
Poland Sp. z o.o., Wrocław

63470758R00066